To: Laura

from my "Kitchens"
to yours,

Barry Zlatopen

29 Kitchens

One Cook

29 Kitchens

One Cook

Barry Zlatoper

Published by BZ PRESS
Honolulu, HI 96802

29kitchens.com

ISBN 978-1-4507-0602-5
First Edition, First Printing—2010

To Zap, Ashley, Michael, David and Amy,
who inspire me to find the worm
that can play a violin.

Contents

Introduction

The greatest compliment a cook can receive after a meal is a request for the recipe. I was the recipient of such a compliment when my son asked me to put my "regulars" together in a bound form for him and the family. Initially, the task looked easy–merely collect a few of my old standbys that have stood the test of time, and print them out. So I began going through my recipe files, which proved to be far more abundant than I had remembered. I reviewed almost a thousand recipes before narrowing them down to a manageable number to meet the requested deadline.

My idea was to keep the recipes as simple as possible, easy for anyone. The "Extreme Enchilada" is an exception to that rule, but I've included a "Shortcuts" version of that Mexican favorite. The more complicated, involved and precise menus I sometimes enjoy serving for dinner parties and guests were left behind in the sorting. I then resolved to make each recipe again, and to photograph the dishes myself. So this was a true labor of love for my favorite people in the world, my family. Then the print-on-demand edition was so popular that I decided to publish a larger edition.

Cooking was not a passion for anyone in my family during my childhood. In fact I only learned very late that "homemade" soup existed. When my husband Zap and I first married he was a pilot on an aircraft carrier, and I followed him off and on for two years around the Mediterranean. It was then that I was awakened to the delightful smells and tastes of all kinds of new foods, though at the time I did not appreciate the transformation that was taking place.

When I came back to the States I started experiments to duplicate the foods I had tasted all over Italy, Spain and Greece. My method was trial and error. My culinary passion became obvious to me one day when a friend asked me which place I visited or lived in had I liked the most. In trying to explain that I'd liked each place for a different reason, I realized I remembered cities by a restaurant and a food I had eaten there: Marseilles for Salad Niçoise, Barcelona for Eggs Florentine in artichoke bottoms, Athens for gyros souvlaki, and steaks with lemon, Corfu for fresh fish fried seaside with French fries and lemon, Sacha's Restaurant in Malta for chocolate fondue and French onion soup, Palma Majorca for open faced tuna sandwiches, and so on.

I delight in trying new recipes and seeing how they turn out. An ingredient may change from a past success, an amount adjusted, or the process modified. This is always a challenge and I enjoy the outcome often enough to make it my rule.

Zap has always been my designated food tester. Every dish is run by him. If he likes it we know it's a winner. He chuckles at the elaborate detail of my *mise en place*, but appreciates the results. For me the whole process of selecting the menu, buying the ingredients, cooking the food, adjusting to my likes and dislikes, preparation and presentation are what make the finished product a piece of art. Each meal is an original experience. Each time it's a new creation. And there's always a self-evaluation; I keep score with myself, as in golf. The better I do, the higher I raise the bar, and the more I get out of it.

Here's hoping you enjoy the contents that follow as much as I did in creating and photographing them.

Breakfast

- Creamed Chipped Beef on Toast
- French Toast
- Fried Tomatoes and Bacon on Toast
- Veggie Bagel
- Homemade Granola

Creamed Chipped Beef on Toast

Ingredients

8 oz. chipped beef pulled apart in pieces

3 tablespoons butter

3 tablespoons flour

2 cups milk

2 tablespoons dry sherry

Salt and pepper to taste

Parsley for garnish

Directions

Melt butter in saucepan.

Slowly add flour and stir constantly until light brown.

Slowly add milk, stirring constantly.

Add the beef. Simmer ingredients until they thicken.

Add sherry and simmer couple more minutes to thicken.

Serve the beef over hot buttered toast.

Garnish with chopped parsley.

Serves 4

French Toast

Ingredients

2 eggs

⅔ - 1 cup milk

½ teaspoon salt

½ teaspoon vanilla

1 tablespoon rum

8 slices of day old French bread

Directions

Beat eggs together slightly.

Add salt.

Add milk.

Flavor with vanilla and rum.

Dip bread slices into milk mixture. Do not leave in mixture too long or they will get soggy.

Brown bread until golden on each side, on hot, well–buttered griddle.

Garnish with cinnamon sugar, and dust with powdered sugar.

Serve hot with maple syrup. Unbelievable!

Serves 4

Fried Tomatoes
and Bacon on Toast

Ingredients

3 medium unpeeled firm ripe tomatoes

$\frac{1}{3}$ cup milk

$\frac{1}{2}$ cup all-purpose flour

$\frac{1}{2}$ teaspoon salt

$\frac{1}{4}$ teaspoon fresh ground black pepper

2 eggs beaten

$\frac{3}{4}$ cup Panko breadcrumbs

$\frac{1}{4}$ cup shortening

Sliced bacon, 2-3 pieces per dish

Directions

Cook bacon.

Cut tomatoes into $\frac{1}{2}$ inch slices.

Combine flour, salt and pepper.

Beat eggs in a bowl.

Dip tomatoes into milk, then flour mixture, then eggs, then breadcrumbs.

In a 10 in. skillet, heat shortening until medium hot.

Sauté tomatoes until golden brown, on both sides.

Season to taste.

Serve over buttered toast.

Layer toast, bacon and then tomatoes, and garnish with fresh basil or parsley.

Serves 4

Veggie Bagel

Ingredients

Red bell pepper, julienne cut

Purple onion sliced thinly

White mushrooms, cut in thin discs

Sprouts

Banana peppers, thinly cut on diagonal

Cream cheese

Tomato, thinly sliced

Bagels

Directions

Butter both sides of the bagels.

Grill bagels lightly on both sides.

Spread cream cheese on both insides of bagel.

Stack tomatoes, onions, mushrooms, red bell peppers, banana peppers and sprouts on bottom half of bagel.

Top with top half of bagel.

Extremely colorful and absolutely delicious!

Homemade Granola

Adapted from Ina Garten's version

Ingredients

4 cups old-fashioned Quaker oats

1 cup sweetened, shredded coconut

1 cup sliced almonds

1 cup chopped walnuts

1 cup chopped pecans

½ teaspoon ground cinnamon

¼ teaspoon vanilla extract

¼ teaspoon almond extract

¾ cup vegetable oil

½ cup honey

½ cup dried figs, small diced

1 cup dried sour cherries, chopped

1 cup dried apricots, small diced

1 cup dried cranberries

Directions

Preheat the oven to 350 degrees F.

In a large bowl mix together oats, coconut, almonds, walnuts, pecans and cinnamon. In a small bowl combine oil, honey and extracts until well mixed. Pour the liquid mixture on top of the dry mixture and stir until dry ingredients are covered well.

Spread mixture evenly onto a baking sheet.

Bake for about 45 minutes, stirring contents around every 15 minutes until mixture is golden brown.

Shut off oven and open door and let sit for an hour to help make it crunchy.

Add dried fruits and mix until well incorporated.

Makes 12 cups

Soups & Sandwiches

- French Onion Soup

- Gazpacho with Crabmeat

- Green Chili Chicken Stew
  New Mexican Style

- Grilled Portobello Mushroom with
  Roasted Green Chilies

French Onion Soup

Ingredients

3 tablespoons butter

1 tablespoon light olive oil or fresh peanut oil

2 cups leeks (white and tender green parts, thinly sliced)

2 large white onions, thinly sliced

2 large red onions, thinly sliced

1 cup shallots, thinly sliced

1 cup green onions (whites only, French cut)

½ teaspoon each of salt and sugar (sugar helps brown the onions)

2 tablespoons of flour

2 ½ qts. homemade beef stock (can substitute beef base or broth). 2 cups of which should be hot.

4-5 tablespoons Cognac, Armagnac or other good brandy

1 cup dry white French Vermouth (can substitute ¼ cup of port wine and ¾ cups red wine)

Directions

Equipment:
Food processor to slice onions

Heavy-bottomed 3 qt. saucepan with cover for onion cook and simmering

Brown onions – 40 minutes

Set saucepan over moderate heat with butter and oil.

When butter has melted stir in onions. Cover the pan and cook slowly until tender and translucent. About 10 minutes.

Blend in salt and sugar. Raise heat to moderately high and let onions brown, stirring frequently until they are dark walnut color. About 25-30 minutes.

Continued >

Makes 2 ½ qts.
Serves 6

< *Continued from previous page*

Simmering Soup

Sprinkle in flour over onion mixture. Cook slowly, stirring 3-4 minutes. Remove from heat. Let cool a minute.

Whisk in 2 cups hot stock and blend well. Bring to simmer, adding rest of stock, cognac and vermouth. Cover loosely.

Simmer very slowly 1 ½ hours, adding a little water if liquid reduces too much.

Correct seasoning.

You can make the soup in advance and keep warm in the oven covered and add liquid as needed or, freeze it.

When ready to assemble, put soup in individual soup bowls. Put croutons on top.

Sprinkle croutons with mozzarella, parmesan, or Swiss cheese.

Dot with oil and broil until bubbly.

Serve with French bread and a big salad and enjoy!

Sauvignon Blanc or Gewürztraminer wine is good with this as well as red wine.

Hard Toasted French Bread Croutons

Ingredients:

1 large 16 in. French bread baguette

½ cup extra virgin olive oil

1 cup grated mozzarella, parmesan or Swiss cheese

Directions:

Slice bread ¾ in. thick.

Spread on olive oil.

Put on baking sheet with parchment paper.

Bake at 325 degrees F 25-30 minutes.

Gazpacho With Crabmeat

Ingredients

2 English or Japanese cucumbers, cut in half and seeded, but not peeled

3 red bell peppers, trimmed and seeded

8 medium red tomatoes

2 medium purple onions

2 garlic cloves, minced

46 oz. tomato juice (6 cups) or 5 cups tomato juice and 1 cup V8 juice

½ cup red wine vinegar

½ cup good extra virgin olive oil

1 tablespoon kosher salt

1½ teaspoons fresh ground black pepper

Dash of cayenne

Jumbo lump crabmeat

Lemon slice

Basil

Directions

Fit a food processor with a steel blade. With a knife, rough chop each vegetable into 1 in. cubes and pulse each vegetable individually in the food processor and then place in a large bowl.

Add garlic, salt and pepper. Stir mixture.

Add juice, vinegar and olive oil. Mix well and chill overnight, at least. Best made a day or so ahead.

When ready to serve, squeeze a little lemon juice on crabmeat and season with salt. Place soup in small bowls and top with crabmeat. Lightly sprinkle cayenne on crabmeat and garnish with fresh basil or cilantro.

Serves 8-10

Green Chile Chicken Stew
New Mexican Style

Ingredients

Nonstick spray

1 teaspoon olive oil or canola oil

3 cloves garlic, peeled and minced

½ white onion, finely diced

1½ pounds chicken breast fillets, skinless, boneless, cut into ½ inch cubes, about 3 cups (Use skinless, boneless chicken breast tenders to reduce prep time by a third)

3 cups reduced sodium chicken broth

1 13 oz. container Bueno frozen Green Chile, not drained (I order Bueno Frozen Green Chile from www.buenofoods.com)

2 carrots, thinly sliced about ⅛ –¼ inch thick

½ cup frozen whole kernel sweet corn (canned is fine)

2 medium Yukon gold or red potatoes, peeled and diced into ¼ inch cubes

¼ teaspoon black pepper

1 teaspoon each of cumin, thyme, marjoram

1 (14 oz.) can of whole tomatoes

1 (14 oz) can black beans or kidney beans

Directions

Spray nonstick sauté pan with nonstick spray.

Add oil.

Heat sauté pan over medium heat for 2-3 minutes.

Add minced garlic and diced onion and sauté until translucent—about 2 minutes.

Transfer garlic and onion into separate bowl with slotted spoon.

Add chicken cubes and cook, stirring until pieces turn white—about 7 minutes.

Add chicken broth.

Add sautéed garlic, onion and remaining ingredients.

Simmer over medium heat until chicken and vegetables are tender—about another 25 minutes.

Lower heat if it begins to boil.

Makes 12 8-oz. servings

Grilled Portobello Mushroom with Roasted Green Chilies

Ingredients

Ciabatta roll

Portobello mushroom

¼ cup extra virgin olive oil

⅛ cup balsamic vinegar

Salt and pepper to taste

1 smashed garlic clove

Mayonnaise (Hellman's or Best)

Mustard (French's classic yellow)

Bibb lettuce

Sliced red onion

Sliced ripe red tomatoes

Sweet and spicy bread and butter pickles

Blue cheese (optional)

Bueno roasted green chilies Hot (www.buenofoods.com or 800-888-7336 to order these.)

Directions

Mix olive oil, balsamic vinegar, crushed garlic, salt, and pepper to taste.

Heat barbecue grill and spray with Pam or wipe with olive oil.

Brush oil mixture on both sides of mushroom, and grill turning once. (About 4 minutes each side on indirect heat)

Butter inside of both halves of roll and grill slightly.

Spread mayonnaise on bottom of roll, mustard on top of roll.

Layer lettuce, onion tomato, pickles, cheese and chilies.

Top with roll and dig in for an amazing treat.

Serves 4

Appetizers

- Fantastic Easy Chili con Queso Dip

- Hot and Creamy Jalapeno Dip

- Parmesan Cheese Puffs

- Seafood Martini

- Tomato Cocktail

Fantastic Easy Chili con Queso Dip

Ingredients

1 small package of Velveeta cheese

1 can of tomatoes and green chilies

1 can of Hormel chili no beans

¼ cup beer

Directions

Combine the ingredients over a double boiler and melt until hot.

Put in a fondue pot or chaffing dish to keep warm. Delicious!

Serve with tortilla chips. Yummmmmmm!

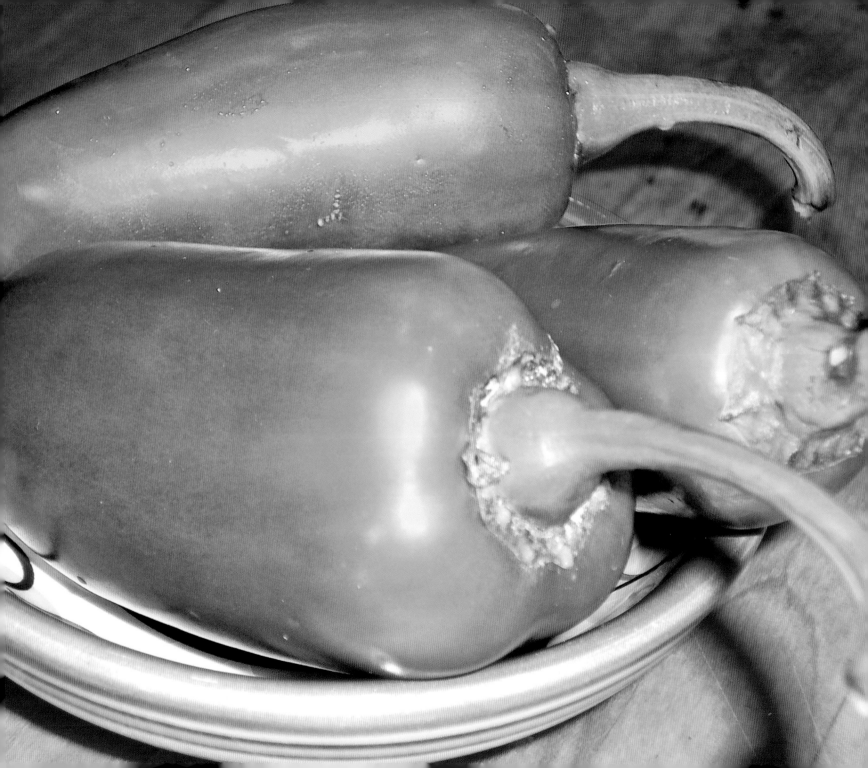

Hot and Creamy Jalapeno Dip

Ingredients

2 cups whipping cream

1 cup sour cream

1 teaspoon chicken base

2 tablespoons clarified butter

2 tablespoons flour

1 fresh jalapeno, minced (or several canned)

1 tablespoon juice from bottled jalapenos (Mrs. Renfro's are my favorite)

4 oz. shredded cheese—equal parts jack and white cheddar

¼ cup beer

Directions

Heat the whipping cream in a heavy saucepan over high heat. When the cream is ready to boil, stir in sour cream. After sour cream dissolves, reduce heat to medium.

Stir in chicken base and jalapeno juice and simmer.

While cream is heating: Make a roux by warming butter in a saucepan over medium heat, adding flour, and mixing with whisk until mixture starts to turn pale gold.

Just before cream mixture is ready to boil again, add roux, whisking briskly and constantly until roux is incorporated.

Remove from heat: stir in beer, minced jalapeno, and the cheese mixture.

Return to heat and stir well until incorporated again. Fantastic!

Makes about 3½ cups

Parmesan Cheese Puffs

Ingredients

6 slices thin sliced whole wheat bread

½ cup mayonnaise (Hellman's)

⅓ cup grated Parmesan cheese

2 tablespoons grated purple onion

Dash of Cayenne (optional)

Splash of wine vinegar peppers (I like Outerbridges Original wine vinegar scented with peppers.)

Directions

Cut 4 small circles from each slice of bread.

Preheat oven to 350 degrees F.

Lightly toast rounds about 5 minutes.

Combine mayonnaise, Parmesan cheese, onion, and wine vinegar.

Top each toast round with mixture, using a melon scoop. (You can freeze puffs at this point and heat when you are ready.)

Bake the puffs at 375 degrees F for 10 minutes, or until the tops are lightly browned.

Garnish with small-diced yellow and red bell peppers.

Great to make ahead and freeze.

Makes 24

Seafood Martini

Ingredients

Cooked shrimp

Avocado

Frisée

Lump crabmeat

Spring onion

Lemon

Directions

Chill a martini glass.

Mix 1 tablespoon of lemon juice with ½ cup water.

Slice avocados about ¼ inch thick.

Dip avocados in lemon juice mixture.

In bottom of glass place some frisée.

Add chunks of lump crabmeat (I like blue claw crabmeat).

Add cooked shrimp to sides of glass.

Alternate with sliced avocado.

Top crabmeat with a tablespoon of cocktail sauce.

Garnish with a lemon slice, twisted.

Top with a Spring onion, split at the ends to flair out.

Tomato Cocktail

Ingredients

½ cup heirloom tomatoes of different colors

Aged balsamic vinegar reduction

Good quality Extra Virgin olive oil

Fresh basil or cilantro

Directions

Pour a cup of vinegar in a saucepan. Put it on medium-high heat and let it reduce until it is thick and coats the back of a spoon. Let cool.

Place the tomatoes in a martini glass.

Drizzle just a touch of the oil on tomatoes.

Drizzle vinegar reduction over tomatoes.

Garnish with a fresh sprig of basil or cilantro.

Salads

Arugula, Endive, and Raspberry Salad

Ingredients

Arugula

Endive

Radicchio

Raspberries

Purple onion, thinly sliced

Pepperoncini

Directions

Tear arugula, endive, and radicchio into small pieces.

Put on a serving plate.

Top with raspberries, purple onion, and pepperoncini.

Drizzle with Red Wine Shallot Vinaigrette dressing.

Red Wine Shallot Vinaigrette

Ingredients:

1 tablespoon of shallots, minced

6 tablespoons red wine vinegar

½ cup Extra Virgin olive oil

Kosher salt

Fresh ground pepper

Directions: In a small bowl, whisk together the vinegar and shallots. Whisk in oil until emulsified. Add kosher salt and fresh ground black pepper.

Serves 4-6

Beets, Orange, and Tomato Salad

Ingredients

Fresh arugula greens

Canned or fresh sliced cooked beets

Orange segments from 2 oranges

Red onion thinly sliced

Toasted chopped pecans,
almonds or walnuts

Vinaigrette

Salt

Pepper

Directions

Wash, spin and crisp arugula greens.

Chill beets.

Toast nuts.

Place greens in a bowl and toss with vinaigrette dressing and remove.

Place greens on a plate and decorate with beets, oranges, onion slices and nuts.

Drizzle more dressing on vegetables.

Serves 4

Dressing Option #1: Vinaigrette

Mix together:

3 tablespoons raspberry
or red wine vinegar

2 tablespoons freshly squeezed orange

juice (reserved from orange segments)

3 tablespoons good extra virgin olive oil

½ teaspoon sugar

1½ teaspoons kosher salt

½ fresh ground black pepper

Dressing Option #2 Sherry Vinaigrette

Mix together:

2 small shallots small diced

2 tablespoons fresh squeezed
orange juice

3 tablespoons sherry vinegar

3 tablespoons good extra virgin olive oil

½ teaspoon sugar

1 ½ teaspoons kosher salt

½ teaspoon fresh ground black pepper

Broiled Caesar Salad

Ingredients

Romaine lettuce

Olive oil

Salt and pepper

Parmesan Cheese

Basil, julienned

1 large vine ripe tomato

Sour dough croutons

Mozzarella cheese

Shrimp

Cornstarch

Egg whites

Red pepper flakes

Sugar

Sour dough baguette

Pesto Vinaigrette

Caesar Salad Dressing

Directions

Wash and crisp the Romaine lettuce. Julienne the basil.

Toss together with some Caesar Salad Dressing, salt and pepper and a sprinkle of Parmesan cheese. Mound on a plate.

Add: 1 large diced vine ripe red tomato, sour dough croutons, shredded mozzarella, and more Parmesan cheese.

Top with shrimp grilled, baked, or fried and little egg white.

Drizzle a little more dressing and sprinkle a little more Parmesan cheese.

Top with Pesto vinaigrette.

Sprinkle bit more Parmesan and mozzarella and run under broiler just to make cheese melt and lightly brown. Garnish with fresh basil.

Continued >

Serves 4

< *Continued from previous page*

Caesar Salad Dressing:

2 cloves garlic minced with
a pinch salt

1 teaspoon Worcestershire sauce

1 tablespoon Dijon mustard

1 tablespoon red wine vinegar

2 tablespoons mayonnaise

½ cup extra virgin olive oil

Salt and pepper to taste

3 tablespoons fresh lemon juice

1 teaspoon of anchovy paste

¼ cup fresh grated Parmesan Cheese

Directions:

Combine garlic, dash of salt, anchovy paste mustard, and Worcestershire sauce in processor.

Add lemon juice, mayonnaise, and red wine vinegar.

Pour in a slow stream extra virgin olive oil until emulsified.

Stir in Parmesan cheese with a fork.

Sour Dough Croutons:

1 baguette

Extra Virgin olive oil

1 teaspoon garlic powder

Salt and pepper to taste

Dash of Cayenne

Directions:

Cut crust off 1 baguette.

Cut into 1" cubes.

Brush cubes with extra virgin olive oil.

Season with garlic powder, salt, pepper, and cayenne.

Put in oven at 450 degrees and watch carefully until toasted golden brown.

Fried shrimp for top of salad:

Butterfly shrimp.

Season with salt, red pepper flakes, white pepper, and sugar.

Dip in egg whites.

Dust with cornstarch.

Let shrimp sit at room temperature 30 minutes. Drain.

Dust more cornstarch and let shrimp absorb it for a bit.

Deep fry shrimp until light golden brown.

Season with salt, sugar and red chili flakes.

Pesto Vinaigrette:

¾ cup packed full of fresh basil leaves

1 clove of garlic minced

½ tablespoon minced shallots

1 tablespoon toasted pine nuts

2½ tablespoons white wine vinegar

½ cup Extra Virgin olive oil

1 tablespoon of freshly grated Parmesan cheese

Directions:

Put first six ingredients in food processor and blend until emulsified.

Add cheese and stir with a fork.

Crab Asparagus Salad

Ingredients

Chilled chicory lettuce

Jumbo lump crabmeat

Cooked and chilled asparagus spears

Cooked hard boiled egg. *See Basics.*

Capers

Vinaigrette Dressing:

4 tablespoons white wine vinegar

2 tablespoons Dijon mustard

1 teaspoon dried oregano

½ teaspoon salt

¼ teaspoon fresh ground pepper

⅔ cup extra virgin olive oil

Serves 4-6

Directions

Steam asparagus for about 4 minutes until just tender, but crisp. Toss immediately in a bowl with ice and water to chill. This enhances color.

Hard boil an egg, cool and then crumble just the yolk. Set aside.

Mix dressing ingredients well and toss the lettuce and asparagus in dressing. Place the chicory on a plate.

Pile crabmeat on top and scatter capers around plate.

Pile asparagus like wigwam poles on top.

Drizzle a little more dressing on the crabmeat and sprinkle crumbled egg yolk around plate.

Option: Russian-type Dressing

½ cup mayonnaise

¼ cup prepared chili sauce (Heinz)

1 tablespoon prepared horseradish

¾ teaspoon Worcestershire Sauce

Salt and pepper to taste

Directions:

Drizzle on crabmeat and lettuce before stacking up asparagus.

Sprinkle crumbled egg yolk around.

Pear, Pecan, and Raspberry Salad

Ingredients

Bibb lettuce

Thinly sliced pears

Thinly sliced purple onion

Candied pecans

Whole raspberries

Goat cheese (prefer Cypress Grove Chevre, Purple Haze)

Parmesan wafer

Dressing:

(Yields enough for 10-12 cups of salad greens)

1 teaspoon Dijon mustard

2 tablespoons white wine vinegar

1 teaspoon fresh lemon juice

Scant ¼ teaspoon salt

5 twists of a pepper mill

Scant ¼ cup olive oil

2 tablespoons of vegetable oil

Directions

Wash, dry, and crisp lettuce.

Slice pears in ¼ inch wedges.

Wash and dry raspberries.

Slice onions very thin. Place pears, raspberries, pecans, onions, and crumbled cheese on lettuce in a fan shape.

Serves 4

Directions for dressing:

Combine mustard, vinegar, lemon juice, salt and pepper in a small bowl with a whisk to dissolve salt.

Slowly whisk in olive oil, and then vegetable oil in a small stream.

Drizzle over salad.

Serve with a parmesan wafer. *See Basics.*

Radicchio and Endive Salad

Ingredients

Radicchio lettuce

Endive lettuce

Celery, thinly chopped

Purple onion, thinly sliced

Chopped pecans, toasted

Dried cranberries

Shaved Parmesano Reggiano cheese

Sherry Vinaigrette (see pg. 49)

Tip: can add Homemade Croutons and/or Goat Cheese Fritters, *see Basics*.

Directions

Tear apart in small pieces radicchio and endive lettuce.

Put lettuce in a mixing bowl.

Add chopped celery, purple onion, pecans, dried cranberries and toss with dressing.

Remove from bowl and put on serving plate.

Top with cheese.

Season with salt and pepper to taste.

Salad Niçoise

Ingredients

½ lb. haricots verts (green beans)

Capers

3 medium ripe tomatoes

1 medium purple onion

15 pitted black olives of your choice

1 can good quality tuna

3 hard- boiled eggs. *See Basics*

1 cooked and chilled beet, sliced (optional)

2 new potatoes boiled, cooled, and sliced or cut into wedges, or 1 can new potatoes chilled and drained

Fresh basil or parsley

Dressing:

¼ cup good extra virgin olive oil

2 tablespoons wine vinegar

¼ teaspoon kosher salt

⅛ teaspoon each: dry mustard, dried tarragon, basil, parsley, garlic salt and fresh ground black pepper

Directions

Trim and cook beans in boiling, salted water until tender and still crunchy. Submerge in an ice bath immediately to retain rich color.

Drain well and set aside.

Boil, peel, and cool potatoes or use chilled can of potatoes. Cut potatoes into wedges.

Cut tomatoes into wedges.

Peel and cut onions into thin slices and separate into rings.

Drain and flake tuna.

Hard boil the eggs and quarter.

To Serve: Arrange a bed of greens on a large platter.

Arrange vegetables in clusters around platter.

Pile tuna in the middle and scatter capers around.

Drizzle dressing all over salad.

Season salad with salt and fresh, ground pepper to taste.

Garnish with fresh basil or parsley.

Serve salad chilled.

Option: Can add sliced green peppers.

Serves 4-6

Entrées

- Boeuf Bourguignon
- Meatloaf Comfort
- Roast Beef Hash
- Original Exrtreme Enchilada
- Short Version Extreme Enchilada
- Sunday Chili
- Week Night Chili
- Spaghetti with Meatballs
- Quick Spaghetti Sauce

- Great Greek Lamb Chops
- Dolmades (Stuffed Grape Leaves) with Tzatziki Sauce
- Barbecue Spare Ribs
- Roast Chicken with Vegetables
- Chicken Florentine

Boeuf Bourguignon

Ingredients

1 tablespoon good olive oil

8 oz. of dry cured center-cut, applewood-smoked bacon, diced

3 lbs. lean chuck roast, cut into 2-inch cubes

4 tablespoons bacon fat, more if needed

Salt and pepper to taste

1 cup of beef stock

2 cups dry red wine

2 tablespoons tomato paste mixed with 2 crushed garlic cloves, 1 teaspoon each of salt and pepper.

Ingredients fo Bouquet Garni:

24 small white onions

24 small carrot pieces, peeled and cut into same size as onions (about 2-inch size)

24 whole fresh mushrooms

Directions for Bouquet Garni:

Sauté bacon on medium heat until browned, about 10 minutes. Remove from fat with a slotted spoon. Set aside.

Dry the beef cubes with paper towels, sprinkle them with salt and pepper, and dredge them in flour. Shake off excess flour. Heat 2 tablespoons of bacon fat in a large Dutch oven. In batches in single layer, sear beef over medium high heat in fat 3-5 minutes turning to brown on all sides. Add more bacon fat as needed. Continue until all the cubes are cooked. Remove seared cubes and keep warm on a plate.

Melt 2 more tablespoons of bacon fat in the pan. Add vegetables and sprinkle with salt and pepper and lightly brown carrots, onions and mushrooms sautéing constantly for about 10-15 minutes. Remove vegetables, set aside and cover. (Sauté a few extra onions for garnish at the end and set aside with bacon bits)

Heat wine and stock to simmering point. Add tomato paste mixture and stir to blend.

Add meat chunks. Bury Bouquet Garni deep into liquid and cover with a piece of tin foil and then put lid on tightly. Reduce heat and simmer slowly for 2 ½ - 3 hours until meat is tender, but not overcooked.

Add vegetables and simmer for another 20 minutes or until vegetables are tender.

Remove Bouquet Garni and season with salt and pepper to taste.

Serve with buttered noodles.

Garnish with bacon pieces, extra browned onions, and fresh parsley.

Directions for Bouquet Garni:

Cut a piece of cheesecloth about 4 x 4 inches. Place 2 teaspoons each of dried parsley, thyme, dried onions, rosemary marjoram, and 2 broken dried bay leaves. Tie up in a little sack with kitchen string.

Meatloaf Comfort

Ingredients

1 envelope Lipton Onion Soup mix

1 ½ -2 lbs. ground beef

1 cup Quaker oats

1 egg

¾ cup water

⅓ cup Heinz ketchup

1 onion, chopped

¼ green bell pepper, chopped

Directions

Preheat oven to 350 degrees F.

In a large bowl combine all ingredients.

In a large shallow pan, shape meat mixture into a loaf.

Bake at 350 degrees F for 1 hour, or until done.

Optional: You can put tomato sauce, or ketchup on top towards the end for color and flavor.

Serves 4-6

Roast Beef Hash

Ingredients

Leftover steak, medium diced

4 baking potatoes

2 green bell peppers, chopped

2 onions, chopped

2 beef bouillon cubes

A1 sauce, 57 sauce, Worcestershire sauce, and soy sauce

4 slices of toast

Directions

Peel and dice raw baking potatoes (or canned potatoes can be used in a pinch) set in cold water until ready.

In a large skillet, sauté onions and green peppers.

Add: 2 cups of boiling water, 2 bouillon cubes, and raw diced potatoes.

Cook covered 15-20 minutes.

Add about 2 tablespoons or more of A1 sauce, 57 sauce, Worcestershire sauce and soy sauce (I add a lot more of the 57sauce than the others because I really like the flavor. You have to taste to suit yourself.) Cook about 15 minutes more.

Add Beef chunks and simmer until the liquid is reduced and slightly thickened, usually about 40 minutes.

Serve over hot buttered toast.

Serves 4

Original Extreme Enchiladas

This recipe has many components. However, there are options included for you to consider. Read all options before starting to decide which suit your need. This recipe can be done with pre-cooked beef, chicken, or pork.

Ingredients

4 oz. pre-cooked, chicken, beef, or pork

2 oz. garlic butter

2 oz. red onions, small dice

3 oz. canned black beans, drained and rinsed

3 oz. canned or frozen corn kernels

1 tablespoon cilantro leaves

Salt and pepper to taste

3 oz. shredded Parmesan cheese

3 oz. shredded cheddar cheese

3 oz. shredded mozzarella cheese

2 oz. Ancho Chili Sauce

1 10-inch flour tortilla per serving

4 oz. Enchilada Sauce

3 oz. Roasted Tomato Salsa (or Pace Picante Sauce instead)

2 tablespoons Cilantro Sour Cream

Directions

Lay flat 1 tortilla and spread with Ancho Chili Sauce on half of tortilla.

Heat garlic butter, then sauté red onions, corn, beans, cilantro, and precooked chicken, beef, or pork.

Season with salt and pepper.

Arrange on center of tortilla with about 1 ½ oz. of assorted cheeses.

Wrap like sushi and place on oiled tinfoil on a sheet pan.

Ladle sauce over top of wrap, and spread 3 different cheeses on top evenly.

Bake at 450 degrees F until hot and bubbly.

Arrange in middle of plate.

Garnish with salsa and Cilantro Sour Cream.

Accompany with guacamole and a mixture of chopped lettuce, tomatoes and onions dressed with oil and red wine vinegar.

Continued >

Entrées

< Continued from previous page

Cajun Spice Blend:

½ cup sugar

¼ cup cayenne pepper

¼ cup black pepper

¼ cup white pepper

¼ cup paprika

2 tablespoons kosher salt

2 tablespoons chili powder

2 tablespoons garlic powder

1 teaspoon dried basil leaves

1 teaspoon dried tarragon leaves

1 teaspoon dried thyme leaves

1 teaspoon dried oregano

Directions:

Mix all ingredients together well. Check for lumps. Place in airtight container and leave in pantry. Use when needed.

Ancho Chili Sauce:

Mix ½ cup ancho chili paste to 1 cup mayonnaise

Cilantro Sour Cream:

(Optional: use sour cream, and have cilantro on the side)

½ cup cilantro leaves

1 cup sour cream

Juice of 1 lemon

Salt and pepper to taste

Directions:

Put all ingredients in food processor and puree until smooth.

Enchilada Sauce:

(Optional: ready-made enchilada sauce)

Peanut oil

1 (28-oz.) can whole tomatoes with juice

2 (15-oz.) cans tomato sauce

Directions for Enchilada Sauce:

In a large pot, heat oil until hot.

Add onions and garlic and sauté until soft. Do not brown garlic.

Add oregano, cumin, chili peppers, and chili powder. Continue cooking about 1 minute.

Add tomato sauce, diced tomatoes, water and season to taste.

Bring to a boil, lower heat and simmer for about 1 hour, stirring occasionally.

Correct seasoning.

Chicken for Enchiladas:

Option: #1: Use prepared South-western grilled chicken strips.

Option #2: Make slow-cooked chicken in a crockpot in advance with *Mexican Verde Slow Cooking Sauce* or *Roja Slow Cooking Sauce* from Williams-Sonoma.

Marinade for Chicken:
The following is the original and takes the longest time:

3 lb. of chicken

$\frac{1}{3}$ cup olive oil

1 teaspoon sambal olek

$\frac{1}{4}$ bunch cilantro with stems, chopped

$\frac{1}{8}$ cup garlic, minced

$\frac{1}{3}$ cup lime juice

2 teaspoons cumin

Salt and pepper to taste

Directions:

Marinate chicken at least 24 hours.

Grill chicken and cut into thin strips.

Beef for Enchiladas:

Option #1: Make slow roasted beef with with *Roja* or *Verde Slow Cooking Sauce*.

Ingredients:

2 lbs. beef chuck roast, cut into 3 in. cubes

Kosher salt and freshly ground pepper, to taste

2-3 tablespoons canola oil

1 jar *Roja Slow Cooking sauce*

Directions:

Season the beef with salt and pepper. In a large fry pan over medium-high heat, warm 2 tablespoons of the oil until almost smoking.

Working in batches (do not overcrowd the pan), brown the beef for 1 to 2 minutes per side, adding more oil between batches if needed.

Transfer the beef to a slow cooker and add the *Roja* or *Verde Slow Cooking Sauce.*

Cover and cook on high until the beef is tender and shreds easily when pulled with a fork, about 5 hours.

Option #2: **Original Beef Recipe**

Ingredients:

1 lb. of hamburger meat

1 clove garlic, minced

2 teaspoons Cajun Spice Blend

$\frac{1}{8}$ cup fresh basil leaves, chiffonade

$\frac{1}{8}$ cup bread crumbs soaked in milk and squeezed dry (optional)

Salt and pepper to taste

Directions:

Mix all ingredients into a stainless steel mixing bowl.

Sauté meat mixture and adjust if necessary. Drain juices.

Option #3: Use 1 pound of hamburger meat, 1 onion, and a taco seasoning packet, and follow directions on packet to cook meat.

Roasted Tomato Salsa:
(Optional: Pace Picante Sauce)

4 tomatoes, halved

1 medium red onion, medium diced

3 oz. olive oil

2 oz. lime juice

1 tablespoon fresh basil, chopped

½ teaspoon sugar

2 teaspoons chipotle paste

Kosher salt and fresh ground black pepper to taste

2 avocados, large diced

Directions:

Place tomatoes cut side up onto a sheet pan lined with parchment paper.

Place into a 400-degree F oven and roast until very soft.

Remove from oven and let cool. Cut into large dice.

Add in rest of the ingredients and blend well. Correct seasoning.

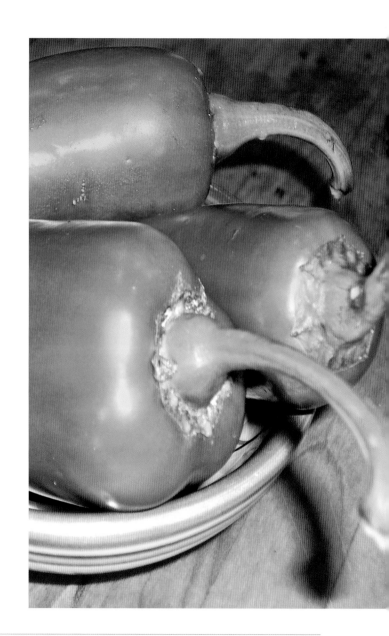

Short Version Extreme Enchilada

Ingredients

4 oz. pre-cooked, chicken, beef, or pork.

2 oz. garlic butter

2 oz. red onions, small dice

3 oz. canned black beans, drained and rinsed

3 oz. canned or frozen corn kernels

1 tablespoon cilantro leaves

Salt and pepper to taste

3 oz. shredded Parmesan cheese

3 oz. shredded cheddar cheese

3 oz. shredded mozzarella cheese

2 oz. Ancho Chili Sauce

1 10-in. flour tortilla

4 oz. Enchilada Sauce

3 oz. Roasted Tomato Salsa
(Pace Picante Sauce instead)

2 tablespoons Cilantro Sour Cream (Cilantro chopped, sour cream separate)

Directions

Lay flat 1 tortilla and spread with Ancho Chili Paste on half of tortilla.

Heat some garlic butter on medium high and sauté red onions, corn, beans, cilantro and precooked chicken, pork or beef.

Season with salt and pepper.

Arrange some mixture on center of tortilla with about 1½ oz. of assorted cheeses.

Wrap like sushi and place on oiled tin foil on a sheet pan.

Ladle sauce over top of wrap, and spread 3 different cheeses on top evenly.

Bake at 450 degrees F until hot and bubbly.

Cut into 2 pieces and arrange on plate.

Garnish with salsa and cilantro sour cream.

Accompany with guacamole, and a mixture of chopped lettuce, tomatoes and onions dressed with oil and vinegar.

Sunday Chili

Ingredients

1½ lbs. ground beef

1 tablespoon butter

2-3 teaspoons salt

1 tablespoon black pepper

1 large onion, chopped

1 (28 oz.) can whole tomatoes,
roughly chopped (use kitchen scissors)

1 can tomato paste

1 can tomato soup

2 tablespoons chili powder

2 tablespoons sugar

1 can kidney beans

Directions

Brown beef in a little oil and drain.

Brown onions in a tablespoon oil and add to beef.

Add rest of ingredients except beans and simmer chili for 1 hour.

Add beans and continue simmering for 1 hour .

Serve over cooked white rice.

Garnish with cheddar cheese, spring onions and tortilla chips.

Serves 4-6

Week Night Chili

Ingredients

1 package of McCormick, El Paso or similar chili season mix

1 lb. lean ground beef

1 onion, chopped

½ green bell pepper

2 cans (8-oz.) tomato sauce and 1 can (14 ½-oz.) diced or whole tomatoes, undrained

1 can (15-16 oz.) kidney beans, drained

Shredded cheddar cheese

Chopped onions, sliced Jalapeno

Peppers

Sour cream

Cilantro

Tortilla chips

Directions

Put a little olive oil in a saucepan over medium high heat and sauté onions and green peppers 2 minutes.

Add the beef.

Sprinkle with kosher salt and coarse black pepper and brown the beef. Drain fat off.

Stir in seasoning mix, tomato sauce, diced tomatoes, and beans. Bring to boil, cover, and reduce heat. Simmer about 20-30 minutes, stirring occasionally.

Serve in a bowl, with or without rice.

Garnish with shredded cheddar cheese, chopped onions, sliced Jalapeno peppers, sour cream, cilantro, and tortilla chips.

Serves 4

Italian Night

Italian food was my premier favorite early on. I always looked forward to Sunday nights in McLean, Virginia when we would do our family dinner. We called ourselves "Momma and Papa Leoni and the Spaghetti Kids" as we made homemade pasta with a pasta machine. Ashley and Michael would hang the freshly made ribbons on the wooden rack to dry while I made the meatballs and sauce. Then after hours of wafting good smells we would all sit down and devour our finished product with lots of pride. We made some really great memories.

Spaghetti with Meatballs

Ingredients

2 lbs. lean ground beef

½ lb. ground pork

4 eggs

2 cups grated Italian Cheese (Romano, Parmesan and Asiago combined)

1½ cups dry French Bread (Bake bread slices at 350 degrees 10-15 minutes and put in food processor)

1 onion, chopped

2 cloves garlic, pressed

½ bunch fresh minced parsley

½ cup milk

1½ tablespoons ketchup

Salt and pepper to taste

Dash of Tabasco sauce

Directions

Mix all ingredients together and form 2½ oz. balls with a #30 or large ice cream scoop, or form by hand. Bake at 350 degrees for 20-25 minutes.

Optional: Sauté in small amount of olive in small batches until golden brown.

Continued >

Makes 30 2 ½ oz. meatballs

< *Continued from previous page*

Sauce Ingredients:

1-2 cloves of Garlic

1 large onion

3 tablespoons olive oil

1 (6 oz.) can tomato paste, 2 (6-oz. cans) water

1 (15 oz.) can of tomato sauce

1 (28 oz.) can whole tomatoes

4 oz. can mushrooms or sautéed some fresh mushrooms

2 teaspoons sugar

2 tablespoons water

Small bunch of chopped fresh parsley

1 teaspoon each of dried rosemary, basil, thyme, fennel seeds, salt and pepper 1 tablespoon oregano

1 celery stalk whole

1 bay leaf

Directions:

Sauté garlic in oil until golden brown, about 30 seconds. Add onions and sauté until tender.

Add rest of ingredients and bring to boil, immediately lower temperature.

Cover and simmer for 2 hours.

Add meatballs and cook another ½ hour at least. Remove celery stalk and bay leaf before serving. Correct seasoning.

Garnish with fresh grated Parmigiano-Reggiano cheese and a basil leaf.

Options:

1. Add Italian sausages sautéed (flavored with fennel is my favorite) and cut into 2-inch pieces.

2. Add Italian sausage split open and meat sautéed and crumbled into sauce.

3. Add sautéed fresh fennel, diced.

Quick Spaghetti Sauce

Ingredients

1–1½lb. ground meat (can add Italian sausage, if desired)

1 onion diced

½ green pepper

1–2 cloves of garlic minced

1 package fresh mushrooms (Sauté in butter separately, then add)

1 stalk celery with leaves (remove after cooked)

1 bay leaf

1 large can (28 oz.) whole Italian tomatoes with juice (Cento is my favorite)

2 tablespoons tomato paste

1 large jar tomato sauce (24–26 oz.) (Paul Newman's Sockarooni Sauce or Williams-Sonoma Sweet Italian Sausage sauce)

1 14½ oz. can tomato sauce (Hunt's or Contadina) or a can of tomato puree and equal can of water

1 teaspoon each of dried herbs: basil, thyme, ground fennel, Italian seasoning.

1–2 tablespoons each of oregano and parsley

½ teaspoon sugar

Salt and pepper to taste

¼– ½ cup of red wine

Directions

Heat pan until hot.

Add coarse ground black pepper and salt to taste.

Add ground meat and onion.

Sauté until meat is almost completely cooked.

Add garlic.

Add green pepper and sauté until meat finished.

Add herbs.

Add tomatoes with juice, jar of sauce, can of sauce, paste and sugar.

Add bay leaf and celery stalk (remove both before serving).

In the meantime, sauté mushrooms in butter and cover until moist and cooked.

Deglaze pan with a little touch of red wine.

Add mushrooms and their juices to sauce.

Add red wine to sauce and cover and let simmer at least 45 minutes.

Serves 4-6

Great Greek Lamb Chops

Ingredients

6 lamb chops

Crushed red pepper flakes

Good extra virgin oil

Marinade:

¼ cup red wine vinegar

⅓ cup good extra virgin olive oil
(lemon olive oil is excellent)

1 whole garlic clove, smashed

Oregano to taste (1 teaspoon–1 tablespoon)

Kosher salt and coarse black pepper to taste

Greek seasoning to taste (1–2 teaspoon.)

Directions

Marinate chops in marinade overnight.

Take out in the morning and place chops on parchment paper on a cookie tray.

Sprinkle chops with kosher salt, coarse black pepper and some crushed red pepper flakes on both sides.

Cover chops with plastic wrap and put in refrigerator until ready to cook.

Bring to room temperature. Brush both sides with extra virgin olive oil.

Grill on high heat 3 minutes on each side (medium rare) or 7 minutes for medium for 1–1½ inch chops.

Squeeze a lemon wedge on each chop and serve.

Let sit 5 minutes before cutting chops to retain juices.

Serves 6

Dolmades (Stuffed Grape Leaves) with Tzatziki Sauce

Ingredients

2½ cups al dente white rice, cooked and cooled

2½ large white onions finely chopped

½ cup spring onion chopped

1 garlic clove, minced

1 teaspoon grated lemon zest

½ cup toasted pine nuts

2 tablespoons finely chopped fresh mint

¼ cup chopped fresh parsley

1 pinch cinnamon

¼ cup olive oil for sautéing

⅔ cup lemon juice, freshly squeezed

1 (8 oz.) jar vine leaves in brine

Marinade (per pan):

¼ cup extra virgin olive oil

¾ cup fresh squeezed lemon juice

Directions

Cook and cool rice according to package for al dente and set aside.

Coat a large sauté pan with ¼ cup olive oil and place over medium heat.

Add the onion, and lemon zest and sauté until soft, about 8 minutes.

Add the garlic, cinnamon, and pine nuts and sauté for 2 more minutes.

Combine these ingredients in a bowl with the cooked rice, fresh mint and parsley and season with salt and pepper.
Set aside.

For grape leaves:
Carefully remove leaves from the jar and place them in a colander to drain off excess brine.

Rinse well under warm water and drain on paper towels. Lay a grape leaf on a flat work surface, shiny side down.

Put 1-2 tablespoons full of filling near the stem end of the leaf. Fold the stem end over the filling, then fold both sides toward the middle, and roll up into a cigarlike shape. They should be snug but not too tight because the rice needs room to swell as it fully cooks. Squeeze gently in the palm of your hand to close the roll. Repeat for the remaining grape leaves.

Once assembled, place the grape leaves in a circle on the bottom of a large sauté pan so they are tightly packed. They can be placed in two layers but not more than two.

Add just enough water to cover the top layer, placing a weighted plate on top. Bring to a boil. Lower heat. Cover tightly, and simmer for about 10-15 minutes.

Add more water if necessary to keep leaves from burning. All the water should be evaporated by then, if not, drain the remaining water. Transfer dolmades in a single layer to flat pans and pour marinade over them.

Place them in the refrigerator overnight or for several hours before serving to enhance flavors.

Serve at room temperature with Tzatziki sauce.

Continued >

Entrées

< *Continued from previous page*

Tzatziki Sauce Ingredients:

1 cucumber grated and squeezed

1 clove garlic, minced with salt

2 cups Greek yogurt

1 tablespoon red wine vinegar

2 tablespoons extra virgin olive oil

$\frac{1}{8}$ teaspoon of dried mint, crushed in palms of your hands

Fresh ground black pepper

Kosher salt

Directions:

Grate cucumber and put in a colander or strainer and press as much liquid out as possible.

Finely mince garlic with salt.

Put all the ingredients in a mini-processor and blend until smooth.

Cover and refrigerate to chill overnight or for several hours.

Amount Per
Calories 5

Total Fat 0g
Sodium 100mg
Total Carbohydrate less than 1g
Protein 0g

Barbecue Spareribs

Ingredients

3 lbs. of spareribs cut in three rib sections

Salt, pepper, garlic salt, or Montreal Bar-B-Q Seasoning, or Montreal Steak Seasoning

1 large onion

2 lemons

1 bottle of your favorite barbecue sauce

Directions

Sprinkle with salt and pepper, garlic salt or Montreal Bar-B-Q Seasoning or Montreal Steak Seasoning.

Put ribs in roast pan bone side down.

Cover with coarsely chopped onion and lemon slices.

Bake uncovered 350 degrees F for 1 hour. Drain off fat.

Flip ribs over and cover with more onions and lemon slices.

Cover with 1 (18 oz.) bottle of barbecue sauce of your choice.

Cover with tinfoil and bake at 300 degrees for 1½ -2 hours.

The meat from these ribs will fall off of the bones and melt in your mouth.

Serves 6

Roast Chicken with Vegetables

Adapted from the Barefoot Contessa Cookbook

Ingredients

1 5-6 lb. roasting chicken

Kosher salt

Coarsely ground black pepper

1 large bunch fresh thyme

1 large lemon cut in half

1 head of garlic, cut in half crosswise

3 tablespoons or more, butter melted

2 Spanish onions quartered

8 whole new red potatoes

4 carrots, peeled and quartered

1-2 cups chicken stock

2 tablespoons all-purpose flour

2 tablespoons of white wine, vermouth, or sherry

2 tablespoons *Wild Mushroom French Finishing Sauce*, from Williams-Sonoma

Directions

Preheat oven to 425 degrees F.

Remove the chicken giblets from inside.

Rinse the chicken inside and out and pat dry. Remove any excess fat.

Place the chicken in a roasting pan. Liberally salt and pepper the inside of the chicken.

Stuff the cavity with the bunch of thyme, both halves of lemon and all the garlic.

Brush the outside of the chicken with the butter and sprinkle again with salt and pepper.

Tie the legs together with kitchen string and tuck the wing tips under the body of the chicken.

Scatter the onion quarters around the chicken. Add 8 whole new red potatoes and 4 carrots, cut diagonally into quarters. Brush vegetables with melted butter. Season them with salt and pepper.

Roast the chicken for 1½ hours, or until the juices run clear when you cut between a leg and thigh (165 degrees F) . Remove to a platter and cover with aluminum foil.

Continued >

Serves 4-6

< *Continued from previous page*

Directions for the Gravy:

Remove all the fat from the bottom of pan, reserving 2 tablespoons in a small cup.

Turn heat to medium. Take pan off heat for a second and add 2 tablespoons of white wine or Vermouth or Sherry to the pan quickly.

Place pan back on heat and add a cup of chicken stock, at first, to the pan and cook on high heat for about 5 minutes until reduced, scraping the bottom of pan to release the tasty drippings.

Combine the 2 tablespoons of chicken fat with the flour and add to the pan. Boil for a few minutes to cook the flour. If it gets too thick add more stock.

Add the mushroom finishing sauce and a touch more wine if you like. Stir to sauce consistency.

Pour the gravy into a small saucepan and season it to taste. Keep warm.

Slice and put chicken on platter and surround with vegetables. Serve gravy on the side.

Chicken Florentine

Ingredients

8 chicken breasts, skinned and boned

Salt and pepper to taste

1 10-oz package of frozen spinach cooked and drained

2 tablespoons melted butter

3 oz. of Peppered Boursin cheese

½ teaspoon real lemon juice

8 slices Swiss cheese

6 tablespoons additional butter

½ cup shredded Parmesan cheese

Directions

Preheat over to 400 degrees F.

Pound chicken until thin; season to taste and set aside.

Mix 2 tablespoons melted butter, cream cheese and lemon juice with spinach.

In the center of each breast, spread 1 slice of Swiss cheese and ¼ cup spinach mixture.

Fold chicken to cover stuffing completely.

Place in a baking dish seam side down and spread 1½ teaspoons of additional butter on each. Sprinkle with Parmesan cheese. Add small amount of white wine and remaining butter to the dish.

Bake at 400 degrees for 25 minutes or until brown.

Serves 8

Seafood

- Cedar Planked Salmon
- Devil's Halibut
- Fish en Papillote
- Scallops with Pernod and Leeks
- Swordfish with Citrus Pesto

Cedar Planked Salmon

Ingredients

4 untreated cedar shingles, about 5 x 10 inches

2 teaspoons vegetable oil

4 (8 oz) salmon fillets, trimmed uniformly

2 teaspoons Potlatch Seasoning
(Williams Sonoma brand)

Hawaiian sea salt

Lemon slices

Seasoned Lemon Butter, recipe follows
(See other options on next page)

Directions

Rub one side of each plank with some vegetable oil, set aside.

Season fish on both sides with Hawaiian sea salt, and let sit a few minutes.

Season the fish on both sides with potlatch seasoning.

Place lemon slices on top in single layer to cover (2-3 slices per fillet). Place a fillet on each oiled shingle. Can prepare ahead of time, at least 30 minutes before cooking. If not using right away, cover with plastic wrap and put in refrigerator.

Fire up grill (have a spray bottle of water handy). Place the planks in the center of a hot barbecue grill. Close the lid and cook for 12-13 minutes, or until the fish flakes easily with a fork.

Remove the planks from the grill using a long handled spatula. If the planks catch fire, sprinkle with a little water.

Top the salmon with seasoned lemon butter or warm sauce.

Place the planks in the middle of the serving plates. Put accompaniments on either side for presentation.

Continued >

Serves 4

< *Continued from previous page*

Seasoned Lemon Butter:

½ lb. unsalted butter, at room temperature

¼ teaspoon minced garlic

1 tablespoon minced scallions (white and green parts)

1 tablespoon minced fresh dill

1 tablespoon fresh minced flat-leaf parsley

1 teaspoon freshly squeezed lemon juice

1 teaspoon kosher salt

¼ teaspoon freshly ground black pepper

Directions:

Combine the butter, garlic, scallions, dill, parsley, juice, salt, and pepper in the bowl of an electric mixer fitted with a paddle attachment. Beat until mixed but do not whip.

To serve, put a teaspoon or so on top of each fillet.

Finishing Sauce Option—Dill Butter:

1 lb. softened unsalted butter

2 oz. shallots (60 grams)

2 oz. fresh dill (60 grams)

1 teaspoon fresh lemon juice

Directions:

Mince shallots.

Chop dill very fine.

Cream butter with hand mixer and blend in the dill, shallots, and lemon juice.

Roll the herb butter into a log in waxed paper. Store in refrigerator, or put in feezer (up to 6 months).

When ready to use, just slice off a pat at a time and put on top of each fillet.

Devil's Halibut

Ingredients

4 Halibut fillets

1 teaspoon Hawaiian Sea Salt

Kosher salt and coarse ground black pepper to taste

3 tablespoons all-purpose flour

1 tablespoon olive oil

½ onion sliced

½ shallot sliced

½ cup pitted kalamata olives

1 garlic clove thinly sliced

3 cups Roma tomatoes

1 cup grape tomatoes

3 tablespoons aged white wine vinegar

1 teaspoon red pepper flakes

1 teaspoon Dijon mustard

1 teaspoon sugar

1 cup chardonnay wine

¼ cup brandy

1 tablespoon Pernod

Lemon wedges

Fresh parsley

Directions

One half -hour before cooking, season fish with Hawaiian sea salt.

When ready to cook, season fish with salt and pepper and dredge 1 side of fillets in flour.

Heat oil in large sauté pan over medium-high heat.

Add fillets, flour side down, and sauté 3 minutes, or until golden brown.

Transfer fillets to a plate and set aside. Reduce heat to medium.

To sauté pan add onion, olives, and garlic; sauté about 2 minutes.

Stir in tomatoes, vinegar, pepper flakes, mustard and sugar.

Deglaze pan with wine, add Pernod and brandy.

Reduce heat to medium-low and simmer until thickened, about 15 minutes.

Gently break up tomatoes with a spoon.

Return fillets to pan, placing them brown side up on top of tomato mixture.

Cover tightly with a lid and simmer 5-7 minutes, until fish is flakey.

Spread sauce on plate. Place fish on top.

Add a drop or two of chili oil to fish.

Garnish with parsley. Serve lemon wedges on the side.

Serves 4

Fish en Papillote

Ingredients

Hawaiian sea salt

¼ cup (2 fl. oz. olive oil) plus some for brushing on fish packets

2 large yellow onions, sliced

Grated zest of 1 large orange

Grated zest of 1 lemon

4 tablespoons chopped fresh tarragon

¼ cup (2 fl. oz.) fresh orange juice

2 tablespoons fresh lemon juice

Kosher salt and fresh ground black pepper to taste

4 flaky white fish fillets like flounder, sole or halibut

2 sheets parchment paper

Can prepare packets of fish ahead of time and bake when ready

Directions

Salt both sides of fillets with sea salt at least 30 minutes before cooking and store.

Preheat oven to 475 degrees F. Fold 2 sheets of parchment paper in half lengthwise. Fold in half again width wise.

Starting at the long fold, cut out 2 heart-shaped pieces from both sheets, yielding 4 heart pockets. Make each sheet about 2 inches wider than the fish fillets. Set aside.

Pour ¼ cup olive oil into sauté pan. On medium heat, sauté onions for about 10 minutes or until tender. Add the orange and lemon zests and tarragon; sauté 3 more minutes.

Add juices and sauté 2 more minutes. Liberally season with kosher salt and black pepper.

Lay hearts on flat surface and brush both sides with more olive oil.

Open a heart and near fold, place 1 fillet on top.

Sprinkle the fish with salt and pepper and top fillet with ¼ the onion mixture.

Fold over paper to enclose the fish. Roll the edges up tightly to seal taking about 2 inches along the edge. Place the packets on a baking sheet. Can store in refrigerator at this point, if desired.

Bake about 12 minutes until the parchment paper is puffed and the edges browned. Cut open a pocket to test one fish with a knife for opaqueness.

Cut open and serve on individual plates. Garnish with tarragon sprig and a lemon slice.

Serves 4

Scallops with Pernod and Leeks

Ingredients

2 leeks, bulbs only, sliced into rings

3 tablespoons unsalted butter

2 tablespoons medium chopped shallots

1 lb. sea scallops

2 tablespoons Pernod

¼ cup champagne

¼ cup clam juice

1 cup of heavy cream

Kosher salt and fresh ground black to taste

Angel hair pasta

Parsley for garnish

Directions

Wash leek rings very well, and dry off with paper towel.

Sauté leek rings in 1 tablespoon butter until soft. (About 1-2 minutes) Set aside.

Sauté shallots in 2 tablespoons butter about 30 seconds until tender.

Add scallops and sauté until opaque, about 2–3 minutes each side.

Remove from pan, cover and keep warm.

Deglaze pan with Pernod. Cook 30 seconds, and add champagne and clam juice.

Boil 2–3 minutes.

Add cream and mix well.

Return scallops to pan and cook briefly to heat up, about 2–3 minutes.

Place scallops on angel hair pasta, drizzle with sauce and top with leek rings.

Garnish with parsley.

Serves 4 as appetizer or 2 as entrée

Swordfish with Citrus Pesto

Ingredients

Citrus Pesto:

1 bunch fresh basil, stemmed (about 3 cups)

½ cup pine nuts, toasted

1 clove garlic

1 lemon, zested and juiced

1 orange, zested and juiced

1 teaspoon lime juice

½ teaspoon salt

½ teaspoon fresh ground black pepper

½ cup extra-virgin olive oil

1 cup grated Parmesan cheese

Swordfish:

4 (6-oz.) swordfish fillets, about 1 inch thick

Hawaiian sea salt

Extra virgin olive oil

Kosher salt and coarse ground black pepper

Directions

About ½ hour before cooking, sprinkle swordfish with Hawaiian sea salt, and let it rest.

Put the basil, pine nuts, garlic, zests, juices, salt, and pepper in a food processor and pulse until the mixture is finely chopped.

Turn the machine back on and slowly add the olive oil until the mixture is smooth and creamy.

Scrape the contents with a rubber spatula into a bowl. Stir in the Parmesan cheese until well incorporated.

Oil grates and preheat a grill. Brush both sides of the swordfish with olive oil and season with kosher salt and black pepper. Grill the swordfish about 3 to 4 minutes on each side.

Transfer the grilled fish to serving plates.

Top with citrus pesto and lemon slices.

Serves 4

Vegetables and Sides

- Baked Beans
- Baked Stuffed Tomatoes Provençales
- Swiss Chards

Baked Beans

Ingredients

2½ cups canned beans (Ex. Campbell's Pork n' Beans)

¼ cup catsup

2 tablespoons barbeque sauce

2 tablespoons molasses

2 tablespoons dark brown sugar

¼ cup onion, chopped

¼ cup green pepper, chopped

¼ cup celery stalks, chopped

2 tablespoons bacon drippings (optional)

3 drops Tabasco sauce

1 tablespoon of French's yellow mustard

2 strips bacon

Directions

Preheat oven to 350 Degrees F.

Pour beans in a bowl and add the rest of the ingredients except the bacon. Stir well.

Place beans in a greased, shallow, ovenproof dish. Top with bacon.

Bake beans covered for 30 minutes and remove cover. Bake another 30 minutes or more until a little thick.

Can make a day ahead of time. Great re-heated.

Serves 4-6

Baked Stuffed Tomatoes Provençale

Ingredients

4 large ripe tomatoes, halved

Kosher salt and fresh ground pepper

½ cup fresh homemade white breadcrumbs

2 tablespoons minced Spring onions

½ medium garlic clove, minced

⅛ cup minced fresh flat leaf parsley

⅛ cup minced fresh basil

⅛ cup fresh grated Parmesan cheese

1–2 tablespoons good extra virgin olive oil

4–6 teaspoons of unsalted butter

Directions

Preheat oven to 400 degrees F.

Cut tomatoes in half crosswise.

Gently squeeze them to remove excess juice.

Dig out seeds very carefully.

Salt and pepper inside tomatoes lightly and turn upside down on rack to drain.

Stuffing:

Toss bread crumbs with onions, garlic, parsley, basil and cheese.

Salt and pepper to taste.

Add small amounts of olive oil as you incorporate.

Divide evenly into 8 portions and stuff into tomatoes mounding on top.

Place in ovenproof dish and dot with butter on top.

Bake in upper third of oven for about 20 minutes until crumbs are lightly browned and the tomatoes are hot. (May be prepared ahead of time and baked later.)

Serves 8

Swiss Chards

I introduce this vegetable because it goes so well with seafood and is very simple to prepare.

Ingredients

1 head of Swiss Chards

1 clove garlic

1 tablespoon olive oil

Salt to taste

Red pepper flakes to taste

Directions

Chiffonade greens.

Mince 1 clove of garlic.

Put 1 tablespoon of olive oil in sauté pan.

When heat is medium high, with a little sizzle, add garlic for about 20 seconds.

Toss greens in quickly, and sauté on medium high, for about 1 minute to keep the bright green color.

Add a pinch of salt.

Sprinkle with red pepper flakes.

Reduce heat to medium low and sauté about 30 seconds–1 minute.

Serves 4

Desserts

- Dark Chocolate Chip Brownies
- Dark and Decadent Chocolate Cookies
- Key Lime Pie Perfection
- Easy Lemon Pie
- Strawberry Blueberry Pie

Dark Chocolate Chip Brownies

My version of Ina Garten's Outrageous Brownies.

Ingredients

1 lb. unsalted butter

1 lb. semisweet chocolate chips

12 oz. dark chocolate chips (Ghiradelli 60% cacao)

6 oz. unsweetened chocolate

6 extra-large eggs

3 tablespoons instant coffee powder (Folger's is fine)

2 tablespoons real vanilla extract

2¼ cups sugar

1 cup all-purpose flour for batter

¼ cup of all-purpose flour for nuts and chips

1 tablespoon of baking powder

1 teaspoon of kosher salt

3 cups chopped walnut pieces

Directions

Preheat oven to 350 degrees F.

Grease and flour a sheet pan (13 by 18 by 1½ inch).

Melt together the butter, 1 lb. semisweet chocolate chips, and unsweetened chocolate on top of a double boiler. Do not boil. Set aside to cool.

In a separate bowl, carefully mix eggs, instant coffee, vanilla and sugar.

Add the chocolate mixture slowly and incorporate thoroughly. Let it cool well to room temperature.

In another bowl, mix 1 cup flour, baking powder, and salt. Add flour mixture to chocolate mixture. Sprinkle remaining flour over walnuts and dark chocolate chips and toss around. Add nuts and chips to chocolate batter. Pour into prepared pan.

Bake for about 30 minutes, or until a toothpick comes out clean when stuck in the middle of pan. Halfway through the baking process, tap the pan against the oven wall and then turn pan around. Cool thoroughly and refrigerate until chilled. Cut into squares. (Can freeze at this point.)

Dust with powdered sugar and serve.

20 large brownies

Dark and Decadent Chocolate Cookies

Ingredients

7½ oz. unsalted butter

1lb. 1½ oz. (17½ oz.) semi-sweet chocolate chips

15 oz. granulated sugar

5 teaspoons vanilla extract

1 tablespoon instant coffee granules

8 whole eggs

4 oz. cake flour

12 oz. all purpose flour

1½ oz cocoa powder

1¼ teaspoons baking powder

7 oz. dark chocolate chips (Ghiradelli)

2 cups powdered sugar

Directions

Over a double boiler, barely simmering, melt semi-sweet chocolate chips and butter together, stirring occasionally. Do not boil.

Using a thermometer, when the mixture reaches 115 degrees F stir in vanilla, sugar and coffee.

Remove from the heat and blend well to dissolve the sugar. Cool.

When cooled, whisk eggs into chocolate mixture one at a time.

In another bowl, sift flour, cocoa powder, and baking powder together.

Pour the dry ingredients into the chocolate mixture just to blend.

Fold in dark chocolate chips and chill dough for at least one hour – but overnight is even better.

Once chilled well weigh 1¼ -1½-oz. portions, using a #40 ice cream scoop. Roll each portion into a ball by hand. Keep dough chilled while working it. You can freeze balls on a cookie sheet with parchment covered in plastic wrap until ready to bake.

When ready to bake, roll each ball into powdered sugar. Place on cookie sheet and bake at 350 degrees F for about 14-16 minutes. These should not be overbaked, so they are chewy inside.

Makes 75 Cookies

Key Lime Pie Perfection

Ingredients

1¼ cups Honey Maid Graham Cracker Crumbs

⅓ cup chopped macadamia nuts

¼ cup plus 2 teaspoons sugar

5 tablespoons melted unsalted butter

5 egg yolks

1 can (14 oz.) Borden's Eagle Brand sweetened condensed milk

⅓ cup 100% real Key lime juice fresh, or Nellie and Joe's Key lime juice

Zest of ½ small lime

1 cup heavy whipped cream

¼ cup confectioner's sugar

Lime slices

Directions

Combine crumbs, macadamia nuts, sugar, and melted butter in a bowl and mix gently until moist.

Put in a 9-inch pie dish and pat crumb mixture with a spoon to form crust to fit dish.

Bake in 350 degrees F oven 6-8 minutes for a crispy crust.

Set aside to cool.

In a bowl, whisk together 5 egg yolks, sweetened and condensed milk, and lime juice.

Pour mixture into cooled pie crust and bake at 350 degrees F for 10–13 minutes.

Cool pie on a rack then chill for at least 4 hours.

Garnish each slice with:

A fresh lime slice and a mint sprig

Serves 6

Easy Lemon Pie

Ingredients

1½ cups sugar

1 cup buttermilk

1 tablespoon of all-purpose flour

2 eggs

2 egg yolks

½ teaspoon real vanilla extract

Grated zest and juice of 1 Myer lemon

1 tablespoon good quality limoncello

Pinch of salt

1 Pillsbury refrigerator 9-inch unbaked pie crust

Topping:

4 cups ripe fresh strawberries

1 teaspoon or more sugar

2 teaspoons good quality limoncello

Whipped cream and more lemon zest for garnish

Directions

Preheat oven to 350 degrees F.

In a large bowl mix well sugar, buttermilk, flour, eggs, yolks, extract, zest juice, limoncello, and salt.

Pour into pie crust. Place pie crust on a baking sheet.

Bake until filling is set, but jiggles in the middle, about 40-45 minutes.

Take pie out of the oven and cool to room temperature. (Can chill if not serving right away. Then let come to room temperature for 15 minutes before serving.)

Topping:

Cut up about 4 cups of fresh strawberries and sprinkle a little sugar and the limoncello on them.

Let them sit for a few minutes before serving. Then place a spoonful on the top of pie.

Top with a dollop of whipped cream (optional). Garnish with more lemon zest.

Serves 6

Strawberry Blueberry Pie

Ingredients

1 Pillsbury 9 in. refrigerator pie crust

1 tablespoon or less creamed cheese

$\frac{2}{3}$ cup sugar

2 tablespoons cornstarch

$\frac{1}{4}$ teaspoon sugar-free raspberry Jello grains

4 cups (1 lb.) fresh strawberries, stemmed (add more as necessary)

2 tablespoons fresh lemon juice

2 cups (8 oz.) blueberries (add as necessary)

$\frac{1}{3}$ cup (3 oz.) raspberry glaze, warm

Directions

Preheat oven to 450 degrees F.

Put fork holes in crust as directed in box.

Bake pie crust 10-12 minutes. Let cool.

Spread cheese on crust bottom.

Hull strawberries with small lemon scoop.

Mix sugar and cornstarch together in a saucepan and add Jello to dissolve.

Pour in 2 cups (8 oz.) of strawberries, lemon juice and stir. Lightly mash berries with potato masher.

Cook mixture over medium heat, stirring constantly, until it comes to a boil.

Reduce heat to low and gently cook for 2 minutes. Remove from the heat and let cook to room temperature, stirring occasionally.

Fold 1½ cups (6 oz.) blueberries into strawberry mixture and pour into cooled pie crust.

Arrange the remaining strawberries in a circle around the edge of the pie and another circle in the middle.

Fill the center with the ½ cup (2 oz.) blueberries.

Brush glaze over the fruit.

Raspberry Glaze:

1½ cups raspberry jam (I use Stonewall Kitchen Seedless Strawberry Jam).

In a small saucepan heat jam to a boil, stirring frequently.

Strain jam over a small bowl.

Reheat clear jam (now glaze) to a boil and turn off immediately.

Use pastry brush to spread on top of pie to make pie sparkle.

Traditional
Holiday Dinner

- Roast Turkey and Cornbread Sausage Stuffing
- Turkey Stuffing Alternative
- Mashed Potatoes
- Green Bean Casserole

- Candied Yams with Marshmallows
- Cranberry Sauce
- Cranberry Salad Mould
- Cranberry Nut Bread
- Smithfield Ham Biscuits ("Hambones")

Roast Turkey and Cornbread Stuffing

Ingredients

12–14 lb. turkey

1 lb. country sausage (Jimmy Dean) cooked and crumbled

1 stick unsalted butter

3-4 ribs celery, diced

1 large onion, diced

1 pkg. Pepperidge Farm Cornbread Stuffing Mix

½ cup fresh parsley, chopped

1 teaspoon of seasoned salt

1 teaspoon fresh ground black pepper

1 tablespoon Bell's Seasoning

1½ cups macadamia nuts chopped

½ cup dry Sherry wine

Splash of peach schnapps

1½ -2 cups turkey or chicken stock

Gravy:

1 cup white wine, or Marsala

1½-2 cups chicken or turkey stock

2 tablespoons Wild Mushroom French Finishing Sauce from Williams-Sonoma

Directions

Melt butter. Sauté celery and onion until translucent (5-7 min).

In a large bowl combine onion, celery, stuffing mix, sausage, herbs, seasonings and nuts. Mix well. Add sherry, Schnapps and enough stock to moisten stuffing.

Put in greased casserole dish at 350 degrees F for 1 hour. Uncover and bake for 15 more min. Serve warm.

Directions for 12-14 lb. Roast Turkey:
Preheat oven to 400 degrees F. Rinse turkey and pat dry. Salt and pepper the inside well.

Place the turkey on a rack in the roasting pan. Brush the turkey with melted butter.

Sprinkle with salt and pepper and stuff the turkey. Roast at 400 degrees F for 30 minutes.

Baste with more melted butter and pan juices and reduce heat to 325 degrees

F and roast for 3½ more hours or until thermometer reads 180 degrees F when inserted in the thigh of the turkey.

Transfer the turkey to a carving board, cover loosely and let rest for about 20 minutes.

Directions for Gravy:
Strain the pan juices into a saucepan, discarding the solids. Skim off the fat, reserving 2 tablespoons of fat.

In a large skillet over medium-low heat, blend the reserved fat with 2 tablespoons of flour, whisking constantly until the flour turns a golden color.

Whisk in the wine and pan juices (1 cup of white wine or Marsala), cooking until slightly thickened, 5-7 minutes. Slowly thin with broth, if needed.

Add 1-2 tablespoons of wild Mushroom French Finishing Sauce and correct seasoning.

Continued >

< *Continued from previous page*

Turkey Stuffing Alternative

(For a 12-14 lb. Turkey)

Ingredients

1 stick of unsalted butter

6 celery stalks, finely diced

2 medium onions, finely diced

1 loaf of French bread cut into 1inch cubes
and toasted, or 1 large bag (13oz.) Pepperidge
Farm stuffing mix

¾ cup flat leaf parsley, chopped

1 teaspoon kosher salt

1 teaspoon freshly ground black pepper or more

1 tablespoon Bell's seasoning

1½ cups macadamia nut pieces or slivered almonds

Up to 2 (14 ½ oz) cans of chicken broth (can
substitute ½ -1 cup of vermouth or white wine for
some of broth). Don't overdo the broth or it will
become mushy.

1½ cups macadamia nut pieces or slivered almonds

Directions

Melt butter in a 12inch skillet over medium heat. Add celery and onion
and cook until they are translucent (5-7 minutes).

In a large bowl or pan, combine celery and onions with bread, parsley,
salt, pepper and Bell's seasoning.

Add broth and wine and stir until well combined. Using a large spoon,
loosely stuff mixture into turkey just before roasting.

Cover and bake any unused stuffing in a greased casserole dish
at 350 degrees F for 1 hour; uncover and bake for 15 more minutes more.

Serve warm.

Mashed Potatoes

Ingredients

2 tablespoons kosher salt

3 lb. Yukon Gold potatoes

½ cup half-and-half

¼ lb. (1 stick) unsalted butter

¾ cup buttermilk (room temperature)

Salt and freshly ground black pepper to taste

Directions

Wash potatoes.

Put them in a pot and cover with boiling, salted water. Bring the water to a boil again, lower the heat and simmer uncovered for about 20-30 minutes, until the potatoes fall apart easily when pierced with a fork.

Heat the half-and-half and butter in a small saucepan. Do no let it boil. Set aside until the potatoes are done.

When the potatoes are tender, drain them in a colander.

Using a potato ricer, process the potatoes.

As soon as they are mashed, stir in hot milk-and-butter mixture with a whisk or potato masher.

Add only enough buttermilk to make the potatoes creamy. You don't need to use all of it.

Add salt and pepper, to taste, and serve hot.

Serves 4-6

Green Bean Casserole

Ingredients

2 cans Delmonte whole green beans

$\frac{1}{8}$ teaspoon fresh ground black pepper

1 (2.8 oz) can French's Fried Onion Rings

1¼ cups American, cheddar or jack cheese, or a combination of all three

1 can Campbell's Cream of Mushroom

¾ cup whole milk

Directions

Drain green beans.

Put in a casserole dish.

Sprinkle with pepper.

Add ¾ can of onion rings and 1 cup of cheese to green beans and mix well.

Mix milk, soup in a separate bowl.

Pour milk mixture over bean mixture.

Sprinkle leftover cheese on top.

Top with onion rings.

Bake at 325 degrees F for 30 minutes.

Serves 4-6

Candied Yams
with Marshmallows

Ingredients

Allow for every cup of potatoes:

1¼ tablespoons of butter

1 tablespoon dark brown sugar

½ teaspoon grated orange or lemon rind

3 tablespoons orange juice

½ teaspoon salt

½ hollowed orange rind

Directions

Preheat oven to 375 degrees F.

Cook and mash sweet potatoes or used canned yams.

Combine the ingredients and place them in a baking dish or hollow orange rinds made into cups, placed in a baking pan.

Sprinkle the tops with brown sugar.

Cover the dish or the cups closely. Bake the potatoes for 30 minutes in the dish or 15 minutes in the orange cups. Remove the cover and top with marshmallows and broil until marshmallows are golden brown.

Cranberry Sauce

Ingredients

4 cups fresh cranberries

2 cups apple juice

¾ cup sugar

¼ teaspoon orange zest

Directions

Place all ingredients in a medium saucepan over medium high heat and bring to a boil.

Reduce to a simmer and stir occasionally.

Cook until the liquid has slightly thickened, about 30 minutes.

Remove from heat, and let cool.

Cover and refrigerate in a serving dish.

Serve in a dished garnished with an orange slice and mint sprig.

Makes 8-10 servings

Cranberry Salad Mould

Nana's Original

Ingredients

1 can (8oz.) crushed pineapple, drained (reserve juice)

2 tablespoons fresh lemon juice

½ cup water

1 (3oz.) package gelatin (raspberry or any flavor), not unsweetened

Dash of salt

1 (16oz.) can whole cranberry sauce

½ cup finely, diced celery

Directions

Mix together reserved juice, water and lemon juice in a sauce pan and bring to a boil.

Remove from heat and add gelatin and salt.

Stir well to dissolve gelatin completely.

Stir cranberry sauce to loosen up and add it to the gelatin mixture.

Chill until slightly thickened.

Fold in pineapple and celery.

Pour all into 1 mold or into individual mold and chill until it sets well.

Serve on lettuce.

Garnish with a dollop of mayonnaise.

Serves 6-8

Cranberry Nut Bread

Ingredients

2 cups flour

1 cup + 2 tablespoons sugar

1¾ teaspoon baking powder

½ teaspoon baking soda

1 teaspoon salt

2 tablespoons melted butter

$\frac{1}{3}$ cup orange juice

¼ cup water

1 lightly beaten egg

2 cups of cranberries

3 oz. chopped wallnuts

Directions

Mix first 5 ingredients together.

Set aside.

Combine next 4 ingredients.

Set aside.

Pour moist mixture over dry mixture and stir until moist.

Stir in 2 cups of cranberries.

Stir in 3oz. chopped walnuts.

Pour batter into greased bread pan.

Bake at 350 degrees F 60-70 minutes.

Yields 1 loaf

Smithfield Ham Biscuits "Hambones"

Ingredients

Pillsbury Buttermilk Biscuits

Genuine Smithfield Ham fully cooked and thinly sliced (I order from www.smithfieldcollection.com in 48 oz. packages)

Butter

Directions

Sauté the ham in a little bit of butter until hot.

Place a small amount in a cooked, buttered biscuit and wrap in tin foil and heat in oven at 325 degrees F for about 5–10 minutes to heat up.

Basics

- Dry Bread Crumbs
- Hardboiled Eggs
- Homemade French Croutons
- Sour Dough Croutons
- Parmesan wafers
- Warm Goat Fritters

Dry Bread Crumbs:

Any type of bread will do. I like French baguettes, or ciabatta bread.

Directions:

Slice bread and place on a sheet pan.

Set in oven at 200 degrees F until they are dry, crisp and golden brown, about 30-45 minutes.

Let cool and then put in food processor until fine.

They will keep for weeks in an airtight container, or better yet, put in the freezer.

Four slices yield about 1 cup.

Hard Boiled Eggs:

Eggs

Cold water

Directions:

Place eggs in a single layer on the bottom of a saucepan.

Cover eggs with 1 inch of cold water.

Cover the pan and put over medium heat.

Let water come to a boil.

Then turn heat off and move the pan off hot burner.

Let them sit in hot water for 15-17 minutes for large eggs.

When time is up, cover in cold water with a few ice cubes to cool eggs.

When they are completely cool, peel them carefully.

If you are doing theses in advance, put the eggs in the refrigerator unpeeled until you are ready to use them.

Homemade French Croutons:

1 French baguette

¼ cup Extra Virgin olive oil flavored with 1 smashed garlic clove

Kosher salt

Fresh ground black pepper

Dried thyme

Dried Italian seasoning

Dried oregano

Dried parsley

Red cayenne pepper

Directions:

Preheat oven to 400 degrees F.

Slice baguette in ¼–½ inch slices.

Spread out on cookie sheet.

Spread oil with a brush on both sides of bread slices.

Sprinkle all dried herbs liberally over both sides of bread.

Lightly sprinkle cayenne on both sides.

Bake 15–20 minutes. Keep a good eye on them and flip over once until golden brown.

Store in container in freezer up to 6 months.

Sour Dough Croutons:

1 baguette

Extra virgin olive oil

1 teaspoon garlic powder

Salt and pepper to taste

Dash of cayenne

Butter

Directions:

Cut crust off 1 baguette.

Cut into 1-inch cubes.

Brush cubes with extra virgin olive oil.

Season with garlic powder, salt, pepper, and cayenne.

Put in oven until toasted golden brown at 450 degrees F and watch carefully.

Parmesan Wafers:

1 cup Parmesan cheese

Directions:

Preheat oven to 400 degrees F.

Take a cookie sheet and put a piece of parchment paper on it.

Use a round shape such as a glass, cookie cutter, disc or whatever you have to draw circles about ½ inch apart. Take a heaping tablespoon of cheese and place in the middle of each circle.

Bake 3–5 minutes.

Let cool and peel off paper. Can stack putting small sheets of parchment paper in between and freeze in container for 3–6 months.

Great for accompaniment to salads, soups and fruit.

Option: Can add herbs and lemon zest for additional savory flavor.

Warm Goat Cheese Fritters
Per Fritter Ingredients

Goat cheese

Panko breadcrumbs

Salt and pepper to taste

Olive oil to fry in

Directions:

Roll goat cheese into balls and shape into discs about 1½ inches.

Bread lightly with Panko breadcrumbs seasoned with kosher salt and fresh ground black pepper.

Fry in olive oil and drain. Serve warm on top of salad.

Sauces

- Beurre Blanc Sauce
- Meatless Tomato Sauce
- Pizza Sauce

Beurre Blanc Sauce:

Serves 4

Add fresh chopped herbs, grated orange, lemon or lime zest to create a sauce that is sensational with grilled fish or chicken.

1 shallot, finely chopped

5 tablespoons fish or chicken stock

5 tablespoons dry white wine

1 tablespoon white wine vinegar

4 oz. unsalted butter

Kosher salt and white pepper

Squeeze of lemon juice

Directions:

Cook the shallot in a little piece of butter until soft.

Add the stock, wine and vinegar, bring to a boil and simmer until it has reduced in quantity to about 3-4 tablespoons.

Keep the saucepan over the heat but draw slightly to one side.

Using a continuous whisking action, whisk in a little piece of butter at a time until all is incorporated and the sauce is thickened.

Season to taste with salt, pepper and lemon juice and serve.

Meatless Tomato Sauce:

1-2 cloves garlic, minced

½ onion, chopped small dice

1 teaspoon olive oil

1-2 teaspoons dried parsley flakes

4 small cans tomato paste (plus 8 small cans water)

1 large can whole Italian tomatoes (28 oz.)

Directions:

Sauté onion and garlic in olive oil.

Put can of whole tomatoes (Hunt's or Cento) in blender and mix. Combine everything and bring to a boil. Lower temperature to simmer and cover. Cook for 15-20 minutes.

Pizza Sauce:

½ onion diced small

1 clove of garlic

2 tablespoons olive oil

1 large can of whole tomatoes

1 small can tomato paste

Oregano (lots according to taste)

2 dashes celery salt

½ teaspoon Italian seasoning

½ teaspoon basil leaves

Salt and pepper to taste

Directions:

Sauté onion and garlic in olive oil.

Put the can of whole tomatoes (Hunt's or Cento) in blender and mix.

Combine everything and bring to a boil. Lower temperature to simmer and cover. Cook for 15–20 minutes.

Yields 1 quart

Index

Notes